Why Do I Nee
Fruits & Veggies?

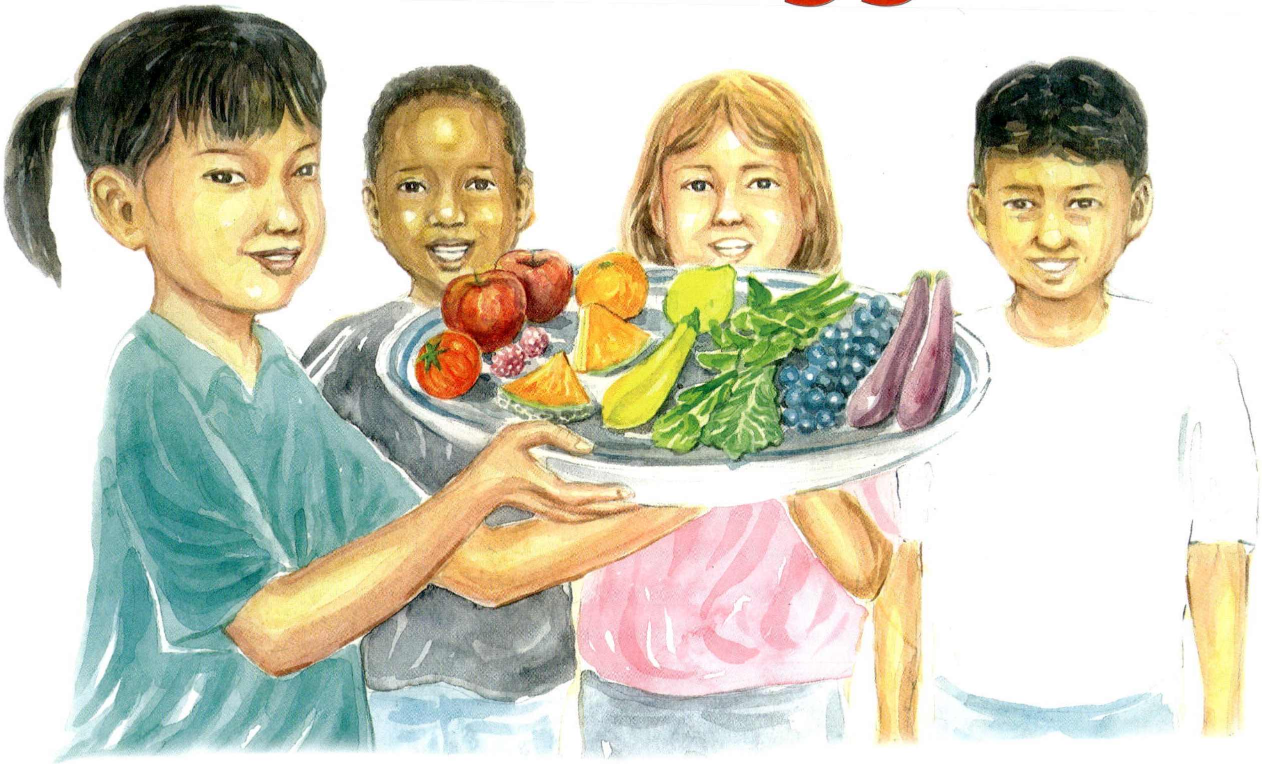

By Johanna Pomeroy-Crockett
Illustrated by Haris Ichwan

Baldwin, New York

“I’m hungry!” said Emily.
“So am I,” Anna said.
“Let’s eat!”

“What do you have?” Pedro asked.
“I have egg salad and some veggies.” said Emily.
“I have a sandwich and grapes,” said Anna.

"What do you have, Mia?" asked Emily.
"What I like to eat," Mia said.
"But that is junk food!" said Anna.

“I like it!” said Mia. “Why should I eat fruits and vegetables? I don’t like them. And, why do you call them veggies?”

"Veggies is easier to say," said Emily. "We learned that fruits and veggies help you grow strong. They help your teeth and your blood."

“Fruits and veggies help you think,” said Pedro.
“They give you energy to play.”
“I still like junk food!” Mia said.

"We have a visitor today." said Mr. Tap.
"This is my Grandfather Ben," said Emily.

"He is a farmer," said Emily.
"He grows fruits and veggies on his farm.
He sells them at the Farmers' Market."

"Today is our class trip to the Farmers' Market," said Mr. Tap. "We will see the food Grandfather Ben grows on his farm."

"I grow food on my farm, "said Grandfather Ben.
"I sell it at the Farmers' Market.
And, I sell it to grocery stores."

"Here we are," said Grandfather Ben.
"This is where I sell my fruits and veggies."
"It smells good here," said Malik.

"Look all around," said Mr. Tap. "See how many different fruits and veggies you can find. See how many different colors you can find."

Lily found red grapes, green grapes, and purple grapes.
Malik found oranges, lemons, and limes.

Anna found watermelons and strawberries.
David found blueberries and peaches.
"Look at the rainbow colors," said Anna.

Sam found red onions, white potatoes, and green peas

Emily found corn and celery and carrots.

Mia found a chair and sat down.

"What's the matter, Mia?" asked Mr. Tap.
"I don't feel well. I'm hungry and tired," Mia said.
"Here is an apple for you," said Grandfather.

Mia ate the apple.
"This is good!" she said. "I feel better.
I guess fruit is good for you."

“Children, come over here, please,” called Grandfather Ben. “Tell me what you found.” The children all began to talk at once.

“Wait, wait. One at a time,” Grandfather said.
One by one, they told what they found.

“I have a surprise for you,” said Grandfather. “Pick out a fruit and a vegetable that you would like to eat.”

"You may take them with you," said Grandfather.
"Thank you, Grandfather Ben," the children said.

"That was fun!" said Mr. Tap. "What did you learn?"

“I learned that I should eat more fruits and veggies,” said Mia. The children laughed.

"Fruits and veggies make your bones strong," said Sam.
"They help you grow," Lily said.
"They help you think better," said Malik.

"They make your teeth strong," said Emily.
"They give you energy so you can run and play."
"They are good for your eyes," said David.

“They are good for your blood,” Pedro said.
“They make your skin nice.”
“They keep you full for a long time,” said Mia.

"They are easy to take with you."
"They are easy to eat," said Anna.
"They taste good," Mia said.

"You should eat two to three fruits
and two to three veggies each day," said Mr. Tap.
"Eat more when you run and play a lot."

“Think about the colors you saw today.
Eat a rainbow of fruits and veggies.
Make a rainbow on your plate,” Mr. Tap said.

“We should make every day a
fruit and vegetable day,” said Sam.
“Hurrah for fruits and veggies!” the children shouted.

About the Author

Johanna Pomeroy-Crockett has spent much of her professional life emphasizing the importance of literacy, especially early literacy which she believes combines reading, writing, art, music, drama and dance. She taught special reading in the inner-city elementary schools in the Southwest and worked in ethnically diverse communities. She also taught reading and academic survival skills at the community college level, supervised teachers in their graduate programs at Northern Arizona University and Arizona State University, and taught reading education courses, including children's literature, at the undergraduate and graduate levels as well as supervising student teachers for Northern Arizona University and the University of Phoenix. She is the author of numerous literacy materials for students and for teachers.

About the Illustrator

Haris Ichwan is a freelance artist. He was born in Solo, Indonesia and studied at the Indonesian Institute of Art (ISI) in Jogiakarta, Java. Haris has collaborated on several art projects and exhibitions throughout Indonesia and the United States. His illustration works also appear in community health and empowerment publications. Haris lives in Washington state with his wife, Jennie and their son, Gabriel.

Book and cover design
by **Tim Homkow**, graphic artist.